MAHIDA'S EXTRA KEY TO HEAVEN

Russell Davis

BROADWAY PLAY PUBLISHING INC
New York
www.broadwayplaypublishing.com
info@broadwayplaypublishing.com

MAHIDA'S EXTRA KEY TO HEAVEN
© Copyright 2020 Russell Davis

Cover art by Kat O'Brien

First published by B P P I, in an earlier version, in
   November 2010
This edition: August 2020
I S B N: 978-0-88145-886-2

Book design: Marie Donovan
Page make-up: Adobe InDesign
Typeface: Palatino

MAHIDA'S EXTRA KEY TO HEAVEN had readings and development work of at the New Harmony Project, National New Play Network, Playwrights Theatre of New Jersey, Epic Theatre Ensemble, and Bard College.

MAHIDA'S EXTRA KEY TO HEAVEN was first produced by Epic Theatre Ensemble from 16 September-18 October 2009 at Signature Theater's Peter Norton Space in in New York. The cast and creative contributors were:

MAHIDA.. Roxanna Hope
THOMAS... James Wallert
EDNA ....Michelle Pawk
RAMIN.. Arian Moayed

Director .... Will Pomerantz
Set .... Mimi Lien
Costumes.. Theresa Squire
Lights ....Justin Townsend
Sound .... Katie Down
Production stage manager ....Erin Koster
Assistant stage manager .... Molly Eustis

MAHIDA'S EXTRA KEY TO HEAVEN was
subsequently produced by Playwrights Theater of
New Jersey, Madison, from 22 April-9 May 2010.
The cast and creative contributors were:

MAHIDA..Mariam Habib
THOMAS...Jack Moran
EDNA .... Jane Blass
RAMIN...Ryan Shams

Director...John Pietrowski
Set .... Drew Francis
Costumes...Sarah Cubbage
Lights .... Richard Currie
Sound ....Jeff Knapp
Properties... Dani Pietrowski
Production stage manager ....Danielle Constance
Assistant stage manager .... Walter F Rodriguez

MAHIDA'S KEY TO HEAVEN was produced at Peterborough Players, Peterborough, New Hampshire, running from 19-30 June 2019. The cast and creative contributors were:

MAHIDA..Aliah Whitmore
THOMAS...Steven Michael Walters
EDNA ....Kathy Manfre
RAMIN..Adham Haddara

Director...Gus Kaikkonen
Sets..Charles Morgan
Lighting/Sound...Kevin Frazier
Costume ....Bethany Mullins
Props ....Emily Allinson
S M...Julia Perez
A S M...Christian Rodriguez

CHARACTERS & SETTING

MAHIDA, *a young woman*
THOMAS, *a young man*
EDNA, THOMAS' *mother*
RAMIN, MAHIDA's *brother*

Several locations in a small town by the ocean
Time: The recent past

PLAYWRIGHT'S NOTE

The punctuation in this script may seem unusual at times. It is not meant to indicate, however, in any way how the lines of dialogue are to be phrased or delivered. It's really about the thoughts, the specific shifts of feeling or insight, and such things can be halting or run together. It's the actor who, according to her or his own dynamic, finds the focus or momentum in those various moments.

an intermission, if desired, could be placed at the end
of Scene Three

Scene One

*(A bench under a streetlamp. Nearby is another streetlamp
and a pier that goes out over the water.)*

*(MAHIDA, a young woman, sits on the bench. She has a
suitcase with her. She wears a long coat, or "manteau". Her
head is covered with a scarf.)*

(It is late at night.)

(Not too faraway is the Canadian border.)

*(THOMAS, a young man, appears. He stops by the lamp at
the edge of the pier. He sees MAHIDA.)*

(MAHIDA stirs on the bench.)

*(THOMAS leans against the railing. He looks out across the
water to the mainland beyond.)*

(He steps back into the light.)

(Pause)

THOMAS: You're not waiting for the ferry, are you?

(No response)

THOMAS: The ferry?
That comes here during the day?

(No response)

THOMAS: I don't think actually there's another ferry.
(Checks notice board at end of pier) There's one tomorrow.
At five in the morning.
(Pause)
I'm sorry. I don't know if you're waiting.

Sorry to bother you.

(MAHIDA *stirs on the bench. She adjusts the scarf on her head.*)

(THOMAS *lingers at the end of the pier.*)

THOMAS: I don't like to be bothered either. I understand. If I'm sitting somewhere at night. By the water, you know. But you have a suitcase, you know. I see a bag there. Somebody supposed to meet you here? I don't know, some time ago?

(*No response*)

THOMAS: Good. I guess I'll continue walking then. Back up to the house I'm staying. Good night, then.

(THOMAS *turns to go.*)

(MAHIDA *quietly weeps.*)

THOMAS: Oh. I'm sorry. I didn't mean to upset you.

(THOMAS *starts to approach the bench.* MAHIDA *stirs in alarm. He halts.*)

THOMAS: Okay. I'll just stand here, okay? (*Pause*) Do you speak English?

(MAHIDA *nods.*)

THOMAS: Well, good. That makes this easier, speaking English. Could you tell me if there's something you need? What might be wrong? (*Pause*) You're alone, right?

(MAHIDA *nods.*)

THOMAS: Maybe I should wait over here, huh? By the railing. Just look out over the water. In case you decide to speak.
(He goes to the railing. He leans against it. He looks out.)
(MAHIDA adjusts herself on the bench.)
MAHIDA: Excuse me. Will there not be a ferry?
THOMAS: A ferry?
MAHIDA: Yes.
THOMAS: No. No, I said so. There's no ferry.
MAHIDA: Oh. No ferry.
THOMAS: I'm sorry. Not till tomorrow.
MAHIDA: Okay.
(Pause)
THOMAS: How well do you speak English?
MAHIDA: Yes, I speak English. I speak English well.
THOMAS: Okay.
MAHIDA: I need sometimes to check.
THOMAS: Check?
MAHIDA: Double-check, yes. I thought I should double-check about the ferry.
THOMAS: Sure.
Sure, I like double-checking too. If I locked the door. Closed the windows. Turn out the lights.
(Pause. He looks out across the water.)
Nice night, huh?
Pretty night up there.
(Pause)
I like this pier. This spot.
I come here a lot when no one else is around.
I like that ferry too. What you're waiting for. I've been on when there's hardly anyone else. Like in the

afternoon. Or now. It would be real nice right now, I
bet, on that ferry. Going across the water, don't you
think, back to the land way over there? Through all this
darkness. This quiet.
I like empty campuses too. And beaches. Beaches are
very good in winter. This town too. I don't know if
you know it, but this is actually a busy place in the
summer. I'd say it bustles. But, you know, I like it
better now. Being out here, wide awake, thinking. Like
some kind of sentinel. Hearing little sounds. What you
don't notice during the day. And what I notice sometimes, I think, is peace. I can feel peaceful, or joy, I
guess, out here at night. Like maybe I notice better that
the world here, all the sky above, is actually probably
infinite. I feel some kind of infinitude. Right in my
thoughts. My chest. I get stirred. And suddenly, you
know, I feel I belong. It's all infinite. There's actually
a huge, invisible space, or ocean, around us. Much
more than what we see. An enormous, inconceivably
large, mental space. All this freedom to move. Which
makes me wonder. How did we get trapped like this,
or educated otherwise, I guess, thinking there was
something, anything, we could possibly ever have such
arguments over? How could there be any conflicting
claim, or fear, with all this immense space between
each one of us?
(Pause)
I'm sorry.
It's hard to articulate sometimes. What I can think.
(Pause)
Do you think I could sit maybe? At the other end of
that bench?

(No response)

THOMAS: No, I guess. I'm probably not much your idea
of company.

(He leans against the railing. He looks out.)
Have you ever been to Wyoming?

(No response)

THOMAS: Do you even know what I mean by that? When I say Wyoming?

MAHIDA: *(Nodding)* Yes.

THOMAS: Okay.

MAHIDA: I know Wyoming is a state.

THOMAS: That's right. A state.
Have you been there?

(MAHIDA shakes her head.)

THOMAS: How about other states?
What other states have you been?

(No response)

THOMAS: Well, my uncle lives in Wyoming. He's a painter. He likes to be alone. I guess I get it from him, this thing about empty spaces. Wyoming, in fact, is where I noticed I have trouble with sleep. Can't stay in a room sometimes. Any place inside.
(Pause)
In Wyoming once I heard a yelping sound at night. My uncle said that's coyotes. They make that sound when they surround a deer that's too old, or injured, to keep up any longer.
I thought it was a horrible sound.
Not what I expect out by myself at night.
(Pause)
I'm sorry. Talking like this about coyotes at night.
(Pause)
Maybe my mother's right.
I should learn how to talk to people.

(MAHIDA stands.)

MAHIDA: Would you like to sit?

THOMAS: Hm?

MAHIDA: Please. You have been standing a long time.

THOMAS: Well, no. I'm fine.

MAHIDA: Well, I will stand then too. Over here.

THOMAS: You're going to stand?

MAHIDA: Yes. I will keep you company. Standing.

THOMAS: Uh huh. What's the matter with sitting?

MAHIDA: Pardon?

THOMAS: We could keep company sitting. Right on that bench.

MAHIDA: Oh, no, I don't think so.

THOMAS: Really, it's quite simple. You'd rather stand?

MAHIDA: Yes, I think so.

THOMAS: You don't like that? If we sat together?

MAHIDA: Well, of course. But someone could see us.

THOMAS: Who's going to see?

MAHIDA: Please. I can stand too. It's my turn to stand.

THOMAS: Okay, well. I won't sit either. I mean, not without you.

MAHIDA: Good. This bench will be our border.

THOMAS: Our border?

MAHIDA: Yes, we have a border, like so, between us.

THOMAS: A border, huh?

MAHIDA: A friendly border, yes.

THOMAS: Well, sure. This is good then, I guess. This border.

MAHIDA: I think so too. We will respect our border.

THOMAS: I certainly will. Anything you wish.

MAHIDA: Thank you.

THOMAS: You're welcome.

(MAHIDA *and* THOMAS *stand either side of the bench.)*

(Pause)

THOMAS: You do speak English. You speak very well.

MAHIDA: Thank you.

THOMAS: Sure.

(Pause)

MAHIDA: It's such a pretty border, yes, don't you think?

THOMAS: What, our bench?

MAHIDA: Yes, I think it's very pretty. This little painted green bench. By the water.

THOMAS: Well, yeah. It's pretty.

(Pause)

MAHIDA: Borders are so peculiar sometimes, I think. What do you think?

THOMAS: About borders?

MAHIDA: Yes.

THOMAS: Well, I don't know. I don't think much about them.

MAHIDA: Oh.

THOMAS: You think that's bad?

MAHIDA: I don't know how you could not think about borders.

THOMAS: Well, of course, I think about them.

MAHIDA: But deeply.

THOMAS: I should think deeply, more deeply, about borders?

MAHIDA: Yes, I think so.

THOMAS: Fine. I'll give it some thought. I will. I'll do some further thinking about borders.

(Pause)

MAHIDA: I think about borders all the time. What is the boundary, I wonder, between what lasts and what does not? What are my real thoughts, and not my thoughts? What is honest, or dissembles? Blesses or curses? What is the boundary, do you know, between these things? What decides? And what possible border could there sometimes be, I wonder, when there is all the infinite space, as you say.
I heard you. How you are stirred.
And so I look at our bench here. It makes me glad. There is a border. A little railing to hold on to. A path to take. Because, of course, someday we can let go. Be free to enter all the infinite space around with no border, no sense of limit. But I do believe, for now, it is important not to let go of this railing we have. It is important not to presume.
I hate it when I presume.

(Pause)

THOMAS: You presume?

MAHIDA: Yes, I'm sorry.

THOMAS: What have you presumed?

MAHIDA: Oh, I presume all the time. I notice it more and more.

THOMAS: Uh huh. Well, I think I'm pretty presumptuous myself.

MAHIDA: Yes?

THOMAS: Sure. I walk around in a state of presumption. This big bloated state. We all do. Little presumptions, profound ones, silly ones.

MAHIDA: Yes, I think so.

THOMAS: Well, sure.

MAHIDA: I'm learning how to be more careful. With my presumptions.

THOMAS: Uh huh. And how's it going?

MAHIDA: Oh. Well, it's a battle, of course.

THOMAS: Uh huh. Any particular presumption?

MAHIDA: Oh, nothing particular exactly.

THOMAS: That's good.

MAHIDA: It's hard, of course, to talk about this. One's presumptions.

THOMAS: Yeah.

MAHIDA: They're so embarrassing sometimes. So fleeting, so personal, so sneaking up on you.

THOMAS: Uh huh.

MAHIDA: And then, of course, there are intuitions. That is very different.

THOMAS: Intuition?

MAHIDA: Oh, yes. There are moments, I think, of insight. Clarity, or compassion. I appreciate very much to have such moments, don't you? I like to be guided.

THOMAS: Guided?

MAHIDA: Yes, I would like to feel so much each step is guided.

THOMAS: By what?

MAHIDA: I don't know. By these moments of insight, I think. This feeling I can have.

THOMAS: Right.

(Pause)

MAHIDA: Perhaps I'm talking too much, I'm sorry.

THOMAS: No. No, I agree with this.

MAHIDA: You do?

THOMAS: Very much, yes. About intuition. Or presumption. I'm glad, really, to hear what you say.

MAHIDA: Thank you.

THOMAS: Sure. You're welcome.

(Pause)

What is your name?
May I ask?

MAHIDA: Mahida.

THOMAS: Uh huh. Mahida.

MAHIDA: Yes.

THOMAS: I'm Thomas.

MAHIDA: Thomas, yes.

(Pause)

THOMAS: Are you waiting, Mahida, may I presume? For the ferry?
Or was someone supposed to meet you here?

(No response)

THOMAS: I'm sorry. You don't seem anxious to answer direct questions sometimes.

Do you come from a land, I guess, where it's not right to ask particular questions? In public maybe?

(MAHIDA fidgets with her coat.)

THOMAS: In your land do you have to repeat a question, I don't know, maybe three times before expecting an answer?

(Pause)

MAHIDA: *(Quietly)* Yes. Yes, I am waiting for the ferry.

THOMAS: Oh.

MAHIDA: I'm sorry. It's embarrassing to wait like this for a ferry.

THOMAS: Well, no, I'm sure there's an explanation.

MAHIDA: I looked too at your schedule.

THOMAS: On the notice board?

MAHIDA: Yes, it said ten o'clock, I thought. I was sure. I was praying this last ferry would still come. It was just late, I hoped.

THOMAS: No, I don't think so. That's just Sunday night.

MAHIDA: Sunday night?

THOMAS: Yes. Lots of folks go back to the mainland late Sunday.

MAHIDA: Oh.

THOMAS: They live and work there during the week. I'm sorry.

MAHIDA: I should learn to read these things better.

THOMAS: Well, no, I get confused by columns too.

MAHIDA: But I presumed.

THOMAS: No, actually, there're lots of people here almost every night waiting for the wrong ferry.

MAHIDA: *(Smiling)* There are not.

THOMAS: No, I've seen them.

MAHIDA: Please.

THOMAS: So would you mind, please, if I ask what you're doing here? Waiting for the wrong ferry?

MAHIDA: No, you should inquire, I know. If I am in trouble. That is courteous and kind.

THOMAS: Okay.

MAHIDA: I understand, thank you. But, no, I am not in trouble, I don't think so. I am just upset now with my brother.

THOMAS: Your brother?

MAHIDA: Yes.

THOMAS: Where is he, your brother?

MAHIDA: I don't know. He left me.

THOMAS: What, waiting for the ferry?

MAHIDA: No, he made me walk. He ordered me out of the car.

THOMAS: You had to walk? From where?

MAHIDA: I don't know. It was a couple of miles, I suppose, three or four.

THOMAS: You walked three or four miles with a suitcase? At night?

MAHIDA: No, it was perhaps five o'clock.

THOMAS: Five o'clock? That's almost dark.

MAHIDA: My brother is angry. He doesn't mean, I'm sure, to be so angry.

THOMAS: I see.

MAHIDA: He wants me to leave the United States. To come home with him.

THOMAS: Uh huh. You don't want to do that?

MAHIDA: Not with my brother, no.

THOMAS: Okay. Why not?

(Pause)

MAHIDA: My brother was not like this before. He is changed. Altered. Now I feel each step I take sometimes, he wants to boss or order. This is upsetting if I am here to get my education. If he thinks like some people now a brother should force a sister.

(Pause)

THOMAS: We don't have to talk about this, you know. About your brother.

(Pause)

You don't have to go home either, you know. Wherever that is. I'm sure we have room for you here. All sorts of room for a person like you.

(Pause)

But don't get me wrong. I'm not exactly a happy member of this country either. In fact, this country has embarrassed me, my country, deeply. I mean, we were talking about our tiny personal presumptions, you and I, but the presumptions of some of the folks who govern, or run our finance, or business, are massive, and I personally believe responsible for how torn apart the world is right now. Making it such a dangerous place to live.

If there's a fire out there, they say, you don't put it out by pouring gasoline on it.

That's what I think.

(Pause)

You want to stand over there by the railing?

MAHIDA: Hm?

THOMAS: Come on. Let's lean on the railing. Look out across the water.

(He goes to the railing.)

(Pause. MAHIDA goes to the railing.)

(MAHIDA and THOMAS lean against the railing, some distance apart.)

THOMAS: Nice night, huh?

Pretty, I think, up there.

(Pause)

I really like it right now. How no one else is around.

(Pause)

Tomorrow will be nothing like this. It'll start to bustle. First thing in the morning. Cars'll line up. All waiting for your ferry out there. Coming from the island further out.

(Pause)

You seem quiet.

Ever since we mentioned your brother.

MAHIDA: I'm sorry.

THOMAS: No, I understand. It's okay.

(Pause)

MAHIDA: I'm just thinking about destiny.

THOMAS: Really, destiny?

MAHIDA: Yes.

THOMAS: What about it?

MAHIDA: Do you feel destined in some way?

THOMAS: Oh, gosh. I don't know.

MAHIDA: You're not so destined, you think?

THOMAS: No, I can feel pretty destined.

MAHIDA: Yes?

THOMAS: Sure, I feel that way. Destined.

MAHIDA: For something great, or memorable, do you suppose?

THOMAS: Well, I don't know who else is going to notice, but I can feel it, sure. Not all the time, I mean, but I get glimpses, I do, of some sort of destiny.

MAHIDA: I feel it too. This destiny.

THOMAS: You do?

MAHIDA: Oh, yes.

THOMAS: You feel it strongly?

MAHIDA: I think so.

THOMAS: Hm. I don't know if I feel it that strongly.

MAHIDA: It's a nice feeling.

THOMAS: Well, sure. So tell me then. What is it, your destiny?

MAHIDA: Oh, how should I know?

THOMAS: Well, I thought you might have some idea.

MAHIDA: I know a few steps ahead, that's all.

THOMAS: Okay, but what about a general direction?

MAHIDA: Well, yes, I'm studying literature right now.

THOMAS: Uh huh.

MAHIDA: At university.

THOMAS: So you're destined for something in literature?

MAHIDA: Yes, I hope so.

THOMAS: Well, I bet you find it. This destiny.

MAHIDA: Thank you.

THOMAS: Sure.

(Pause)

MAHIDA: What about your destiny? Your general direction?

THOMAS: Well, I'm hoping I'm destined probably to be a painter.

MAHIDA: You will be a painter?

THOMAS: Yeah, I'm kind of at loose ends right now. This is hard. I'm wondering if I have to go back to school, some kind of graduate program, to be a painter.

MAHIDA: Oh, yes.

THOMAS: What do you think? Should I go to graduate school, or just set out on my own?

MAHIDA: Oh, dear, I would have no opinion.

THOMAS: Sure, you do.

MAHIDA: How could I have an opinion? I know nothing of your painting. Or of such a graduate school.

THOMAS: Well, you might have a feeling, I bet, about my destiny. What direction to take.

MAHIDA: No, I'm afraid I would be very misleading.

THOMAS: No, I can't imagine that, you misleading.

MAHIDA: I'm terrible, I'm sorry, with advice.

THOMAS: No way.

MAHIDA: Please, you must never believe any advice I give.

THOMAS: Why, what happens to people who heed your advice?

MAHIDA: They come to no good, I'm sure.

THOMAS: I can't imagine that.

MAHIDA: Well, hopefully you will not have to learn the hard way.

THOMAS: I'm always learning the hard way. I can't seem to help myself.

MAHIDA: Oh, dear, well, me too.

THOMAS: You learn things the hard way?

MAHIDA: I think so.

THOMAS: That can't be true.

MAHIDA: Of course, it is.

THOMAS: No, a person who learns the hard way looks exactly like me. All tussled and disheveled.

MAHIDA: You are not disheveled.

THOMAS: Sure, I am. I feel it all the time.

MAHIDA: Oh, stop.

THOMAS: No, I'm disheveled. And you are not. You're actually rather prim, you know. And proper.

MAHIDA: I'm proper?

THOMAS: Yes, I can feel a properness in you.

MAHIDA: I'm sorry.

THOMAS: No, it's very nice, this properness. It's restrained, it's quiet. It's actually rather ethereal.

MAHIDA: Oh?

THOMAS: Yes, this properness you have, it's ethereal, I think. Otherworldly.

MAHIDA: Well, thank you. You too are ethereal yourself.

THOMAS: No, I'm not, come on. I'm tussled and disheveled. I'm dirt poor.

MAHIDA: That can be ethereal.

THOMAS: Nope. I'm not ethereal.

MAHIDA: Yes, you are, I know.

THOMAS: You probably don't even know what that word means, you're using it so wrong.

MAHIDA: I know the word ethereal. I use it very correctly.

THOMAS: Pah.

MAHIDA: Fine. I'm not ethereal either.

THOMAS: Good. We're both ordinary then. Not a shred of destiny.

MAHIDA: Yes.

(Pause)

THOMAS: I'm just teasing.

MAHIDA: Yes, I know.

THOMAS: You're very tempting to tease.

MAHIDA: Thank you.

THOMAS: Sure.

(Pause)

You're not expecting, are you, to stay out here all night? Till that ferry comes?

(Pause)

You know there's no hotel, really, or inn, this time of the year? Nothing that's open.

(Pause)

Look. You can't stay out here. There's no way. I can take you to my mother's. I'm visiting my mother's. She wouldn't mind. She's asleep. I can set you up on the couch.

Would you like to meet my mother? Stay overnight with her?

(MAHIDA goes back to the bench. She stands by it.)

MAHIDA: I don't know. Thank you.

THOMAS: No?

MAHIDA: I'm concerned, no, about my brother.

THOMAS: Concerned?

MAHIDA: He's upset, yes. He could still be somewhere.

THOMAS: What, on the island?

MAHIDA: I don't know.

THOMAS: Oh.

MAHIDA: He probably has taken the last ferry, I'm sure, but perhaps not. I can't be sure if my brother is not in the darkness somewhere. Perhaps watching me. Maybe over there by the buildings.

THOMAS: *(Uncomfortable)* Oh?

MAHIDA: In the shadows, yes, I don't know.

(Pause)

MAHIDA: I'm sorry. It's upsetting, as I say, I have been two years in this country, this is embarrassing.

THOMAS: No, it's just a problem. A legitimate problem.

MAHIDA: I'm sorry.

THOMAS: Look, you think you're embarrassed? I offered to introduce you to my mother.

MAHIDA: I can't go to your mother's.

THOMAS: Why? You're going to stay out here?

MAHIDA: Yes, I think so. If I stay out here in the open.

THOMAS: What, you'd sit up all night on a bench in the cold for your brother? In case he's somewhere? Lurking in the darkness.

MAHIDA: I don't know.

(THOMAS goes to the bench. He sits at one end.)

THOMAS: I'm going to sit here, for a moment, on our border.

(Pause)

(Quietly) What the hell is troubling your brother?

(Pause. MAHIDA stands by her suitcase near the bench.)

MAHIDA: My brother showed up at my dormitory this morning. I did not know he was in this country. It was a shock to me. And then he packed this bag. Put everything he thought I should have and took it out to the car. And I thought, sure, he can take what's in that bag. To the airport, or wherever he expects we should go. I'm staying here. And then I thought, no, something's wrong. There must be some trouble I don't know. We should talk. We'll talk together in this rented car. So I got in and suggested, Come, Ramin, let's take that ferry. A boat going nowhere. And so we sat on the deck, talking. And when the ferry landed, we went for a drive. I was so hopeful we could begin again to understand each other, to be so close and proud to be with each other.

But it became impossible all over.

My brother thinks because our father has died, he must now be in charge. Command what I must do. But it is my father who sent me here. Instructed me to finish university. I want to follow my father's wishes. Not what my brother now decides.

(Pause)

My brother left me abandoned on this island. To make my own way back to school.

Or else he is watching somewhere, over there, waiting to see how I will handle this.

(Pause)

I could, of course, go over there somewhere and call out, Ramin. Ramin, please help me. I am a woman all alone, I know, in the world. Your sister. Please, come out and be nice.

But he will only take it as a sign I will go back with him.

(THOMAS gets up from the bench.)

THOMAS: I think what I want to do is tell you how to get to my mother's house. It's not far.

Would you let me tell you?

(No response)

THOMAS: You walk this way along the water. Past the end of the square. The first street on the left is Pleasant Lane. My mother lives there. Number ten. Okay? You go up the steps of number ten and let yourself in the front door. It's not locked. My mother has this thing about locking, but I didn't lock it.

(Pause)
So I'm going to start walking, okay? Take a different way home. And you should probably hang out here for awhile. Half an hour maybe. Then just get up like you're going for a walk. Make your way to number ten Pleasant Lane.

(Pause)
If you're not going to do this, tell me. And I'll stay here. Over by the railing and keep watch or something while you rest on this bench. I'm good at this. I can keep watch all night.

(Pause)
I have to head back to the mainland myself. We can talk about that tomorrow. About getting you where you have to go. Your university.

MAHIDA: Thank you.

THOMAS: You're welcome.

(Pause)
Should I leave you here?

MAHIDA: Yes.

THOMAS: You're going to my mother's?

MAHIDA: Number ten Pleasant Land. Yes.

THOMAS: Okay. Good, then.
(He lingers. He looks out across the water.)
My mother's going to tell you I don't talk.

MAHIDA: Pardon?

THOMAS: My mother insists I'm a lousy talker. Talking's important to her. She says I'm surly. Just warning you.

MAHIDA: Surly?

THOMAS: Yes, but you can tell her tomorrow that's not true. You heard me talk.

MAHIDA: Yes.

THOMAS: You've seen the talker in me.

MAHIDA: Yes, I did. Thank you.

THOMAS: Sure. You're very welcome.
(He bows. He heads off, walking.)

(MAHIDA sits on the bench. She listens. She looks warily into the distance.)

Scene Two

(A living room. The next morning)

(MAHIDA is asleep under a blanket on the couch.)

(EDNA stands at the bottom of a staircase. She holds a note. She regards MAHIDA on the couch. She looks at the note. She regards MAHIDA's suitcase nearby.)

(She goes to the couch. She looks down at MAHIDA's shoes. They are arranged side by side so that the heel of one shoe is lined up with the toe of the other. EDNA reaches down and rearranges them so the toes are pointing in the same direction.)

(MAHIDA stirs.)

(EDNA sits in a chair.)

(MAHIDA sits up, dazed. She sees EDNA.)

MAHIDA: Oh. I'm sorry.

EDNA: Good morning.

MAHIDA: Yes, good morning. I'm so sorry.

EDNA: About what?

MAHIDA: To be in your house. Like so.

EDNA: It's all right. This note was left on my door. It says you're from Iran.

MAHIDA: Yes. Yes, I am.

EDNA: Iran, huh? It says you missed your ferry.

MAHIDA: Yes, I'm sorry.

EDNA: Couldn't read the schedule, no?

MAHIDA: No, I don't think so.

EDNA: How long have you been in this country?

MAHIDA: I have been two years now. At university.

EDNA: I see.

MAHIDA: Yes.

EDNA: And what do you study?

MAHIDA: Literature.

EDNA: Really? Iranian literature?

MAHIDA: No, just literature. All kinds.

EDNA: Oh. You're a good student, I expect?

MAHIDA: Well, I have to work hard, yes. The university sponsored me to come to this country to study.

EDNA: You were sponsored, huh?

MAHIDA: Oh, yes. My father had to obtain many letters, or affidavits, from business connections, particularly in this country.

EDNA: I see.

MAHIDA: It took quite a long time.

EDNA: So now you're here, yes, for literature?

MAHIDA: Yes, I am.

EDNA: And what is it you're going to do with all this literature?

MAHIDA: I hope someday, I think, to be a writer.

EDNA: Oh?

MAHIDA: Yes, I would like to be a novelist, I believe.

EDNA: Well, I guess you better get married.

MAHIDA: Oh?

EDNA: There's not much dependable income in novels.

MAHIDA: Well, of course, it can be a struggle.

EDNA: Take a look at my son.

MAHIDA: Your son is a writer?

EDNA: No, he has plans, I think, to be a painter. He fancies his uncle.

MAHIDA: Yes.

EDNA: You know about his uncle?

MAHIDA: Well, he told me. A little.

EDNA: Uh huh. Well, I'm glad he told you a little. He doesn't tell me a thing.

MAHIDA: No?

EDNA: Oh, no. He's quite surly around here.

MAHIDA: Really?

EDNA: Yes, not at all respectful. Or helpful.

MAHIDA: How could that be? He seems such a gentleman.

EDNA: A gentleman?

MAHIDA: Oh, yes.

EDNA: I've never seen that. My son the gentleman.

MAHIDA: I'm sorry.

EDNA: Yes, he doesn't know at all how to talk to his mother. How to keep company. I mean, he comes here, what, maybe once a year and stands around, restless, and then has nothing to say. Not a word. I ask about his friends, those folks at school. If anyone's married now. Any babies. Who's doing what kind of job, contributing, you know, to the workings of our

country. This great land. And he gets surly. This is not
communication, he says, this conversation. Who cares
if people are married, who has a toddler now, a dog,
or making lots of contribution to the land? And I say,
How can you talk like that? How can you say, Who
cares? And he says, Mother, stop. I'm trying to figure
out, really, something else. And I say, What else? What
else is there to figure? How do you expect to get by
in this world? You're turning into a good for nothing.
You'll not be any painter. No Rembrandt or Monet. I've
seen what you work on. The most you'll do is paint
houses, if they allow that. Because frankly you can't go
painting houses in the middle of the night the way you
don't sleep. It's unnerving to have a son around who
doesn't know how to sleep and who's always off in a
corner by himself.

(Pause)

How's the weather in Iran?

MAHIDA: The weather?

EDNA: Yes, I hear it can be very hot over there.

MAHIDA: Yes, it's hot. But also very cold.

EDNA: Really?

MAHIDA: Yes, we have mountains and very cold
winters. As well as deserts.

EDNA: Well, we have those here too. Deserts.

MAHIDA: Yes.

EDNA: Our deserts are hot.

MAHIDA: Yes.

EDNA: Are you intending then to marry an Iranian?
A husband who will let you write? Do they do that in
Iran? Do they let you write?

MAHIDA: I'm not sure, no, of my plans now.

EDNA: Or are you actually thinking of staying here in this country?

MAHIDA: I'm just planning, first, on learning to write.

EDNA: Well, actually, I'm sure we could use a translator. There's a desperate need for that. Lots of translating, I've heard.

MAHIDA: Yes, I can translate.

EDNA: Well, good, then. You'll probably be fine.

MAHIDA: I hope so, yes.

EDNA: Do you have any brothers or sisters? I hear families are large over there in the Middle East.

MAHIDA: Oh, yes. In fact, my brother is here.

EDNA: Really?

MAHIDA: Yes, it is a complete surprise to me. He says our father applied for him sometime ago to visit this country. They have a lottery for this at the Swiss Embassy in Tehran.

EDNA: Oh, your brother won a lottery?

MAHIDA: Yes. I believe so. He has been attending the University of Science and Technology in Tehran.

EDNA: Oh, yes, over there?

MAHIDA: Yes, he was hoping one time, I know, to attend a religious school. Perhaps in Qom, we thought, but my father thought that was silly. My brother doesn't know how to apply himself.

EDNA: Ah, religious? He wanted one of those madrassas, I expect.

MAHIDA: No, actually, we don't have those in Iran. Madrassas.

EDNA: No? Well, one of those places, you know, where they learn to memorize the Koran, I hear. Make fatwas or something, lots of car bombs.

MAHIDA: Pardon?

EDNA: Listen, I'm sorry, by the way. About all that stuff going on over there in the Middle East. All that turmoil. The fuss and bother. We're trying to do our best, you know.

MAHIDA: I understand.

EDNA: Our politicians, all our soldiers. Our best. We're trying to ease your transition into the modern world.

MAHIDA: Thank you, yes.

EDNA: Or postmodern, whatever they call it now. It's just such a problem sometimes, don't you think, catching up? What a business. After all these centuries. Africa, the Middle East. Only the Asians. The Asians seem rather good, I think, at catching up. Sometimes, actually, I wish my son were Asian. They have a good work ethic. Good family practice. My son should study Asian, probably, since this country obviously doesn't seem to work for him. He's quite critical, you know. It's appalling.

MAHIDA: He criticizes this country?

EDNA: Oh, yes, right to my face. Or he doesn't actually criticize. He's just surly. Gets surly when I bring up the subject of our country. There're very few subjects I can bring up that won't make him surly. I can't think of one. It's quite distressing.
(Pause)
He talked last night, you say?

MAHIDA: Yes.

EDNA: About what?

MAHIDA: Oh, well, we talked about how pretty it is at night. How quiet. Or infinite. Also about destiny, intuitions. About presumptions. We do not want to have presumptions, either of us.

EDNA: Presumptions?

MAHIDA: Yes, we do not want to presume.

EDNA: Presume what, may I ask?

MAHIDA: Oh, just anything. About ourselves. About other people. About what's real or not real.

EDNA: This is what my son talks about?

MAHIDA: Oh, yes.

EDNA: Real and not real?

MAHIDA: Well, I think so.

EDNA: He already knows what's real. He's been told. What's he talking like that for?

MAHIDA: He's thinking.

EDNA: Thinking, is he? You call that thinking?

MAHIDA: Yes, I do.

EDNA: Listen, I think you should be a little more careful. Don't they teach you in Iran to be careful about men?

MAHIDA: Yes?

EDNA: Well, you don't want to get tangled up in what Thomas considers thinking. It's not thinking at all. It's balderdash. Makes him surly, all this thinking. You seem like a perfectly nice Middle Eastern woman and you're going to turn out surly yourself if you have much more to do with Thomas, I warn you.

MAHIDA: Okay.

EDNA: Good, then. Because I can tell, as a mother, you seem to like him. He's been respectful or something to you. And he left this nicely written note. Invited you here on this couch. And I want to make the best for my son, I do, but mixing cultures between a man and a woman is a bad thing. It leads to no good, I know, unless you happen to be Asian, and even then it's still mostly a problem. It has to be.

MAHIDA: Okay.

EDNA: Well, good. That's said.

I imagine you want some breakfast. I'll make you breakfast so we can get you back to that university on the mainland.

Would an omelette be good for you?

MAHIDA: Yes?

EDNA: A cheese omelette with toast? And juice?

MAHIDA: Yes, thank you.

EDNA: Good. I'll let you get ready.
(She exits through the dining room door.)

(MAHIDA looks down at her shoes. She sees they've been rearranged. She puts them back the way they were before: heels lined up with toes.)

(THOMAS appears on the staircase. He knocks on the balustrade.)

THOMAS: I'm sorry.

MAHIDA: *(Turning)* Pardon?

THOMAS: Real sorry. I heard my mother just now. From the stairs.

MAHIDA: Oh, I don't mind.

THOMAS: May I come in?

MAHIDA: Of course.

(THOMAS steps into the room.)

THOMAS: *(Restless)* I keep forgetting how embarrassing this is. But I can't suppress it. There's no point trying to suppress what my mother has to say. You're just going to have to hear. Until we get you out. The next ferry leaves in forty minutes, so we should eat pretty soon.

MAHIDA: Okay, yes.

THOMAS: I'm really not surly, you know that? I promise.

MAHIDA: I understand.

THOMAS: I mean, I obviously fall silent. If I can't think and talk all at once like she does.

MAHIDA: No, myself too.

THOMAS: I have those moments, sure. Especially around here. Because she confuses me, my mother. I don't understand, frankly, how we're related. What the underlying, unseen similarity is. But that's not surly.

MAHIDA: Please. I think it's funny, actually, your mother.

THOMAS: You do?

MAHIDA: Yes, I giggled a little.

THOMAS: Giggled?

MAHIDA: Inside, yes. It's not a problem, I can tell. In a couple of years I think you and your mother will be fine. You might learn to talk to her, who knows, and she could learn to listen.

THOMAS: *(Doubtful)* This is so hopeful.

MAHIDA: Never give up on a mother. It is unwise.

THOMAS: Unwise?

MAHIDA: Yes, you may be destined to have her all over again.

THOMAS: What do you mean, destined all over?

MAHIDA: If there is a next life, I think so.

THOMAS: I could have to do this again?

MAHIDA: It could be.

THOMAS: Fine. I'll not be surly.

MAHIDA: Good.

THOMAS: I'll figure out a way to talk.

MAHIDA: I think so.

THOMAS: Maybe I should just smile more often, that's all, in this house. Smile. Not be so perturbed and particular. So eager to get out.
(He regards the room.)
I don't know. Maybe we should stick around a little. Take a later ferry. Not rush like this, huh? Maybe take a walk outside.

MAHIDA: Yes?

(EDNA appears at the dining room door.)

EDNA: Thomas?

THOMAS: Yes, Mother?

EDNA: Are you ready too for breakfast?

THOMAS: Yes, of course. I'd like that. *(Smiling)* Breakfast.

EDNA: Well, it's almost ready. We're having omelettes and toast.

THOMAS: Thank you, Mother.

EDNA: Oh, dear.

(EDNA goes to the couch. She looks down at MAHIDA's shoes.)

EDNA: It's really quite odd, what you seem to do with your shoes.

(EDNA *reaches down and rearranges* MAHIDA's *shoes so the toes and heels are lined up together again.*)

EDNA: Is this some sort of Middle Eastern practice here you do with your shoes, putting them like that?

MAHIDA: I'm sorry.

EDNA: No, really, it's an odd practice. Is it cultural?

MAHIDA: It's not cultural, no.

EDNA: You know, I like things just so in this house.

MAHIDA: I've always done this since I was a child.

EDNA: What, put your shoes like that?

MAHIDA: Yes.

THOMAS: (*Smiling*) Mother, what are you talking about?

MAHIDA: I put my shoes like so, with the heel and toe together, because I don't like to presume to know which way I will go when I step back into my shoes.

EDNA: Oh?

MAHIDA: When I wake up, yes, in the morning.

EDNA: I see. Well, shoes go like this, like so, in this house. Everyone should know which way they're going when they get up. At least in my house. Outside of my house you can do as you please. But in here we all know where we go.

Right, Thomas?

THOMAS: (*Smiling*) Uh huh.

(EDNA *exits through the dining room door.*)

(*Pause.* THOMAS *kneels down. He rearranges the shoes so they are lined up toe to heel again.*)

THOMAS: I'll join you in the kitchen.

MAHIDA: Okay.

THOMAS: Good. I'll see you there.

(He exits to the staircase.)

(MAHIDA puts on her shoes. She looks out the window.)

Scene Three

(A back porch. Later that morning)

(MAHIDA sits, reading through a sheaf of papers in her lap.)

(THOMAS comes out onto the porch. MAHIDA looks up.)

(Pause)

THOMAS: What are you reading?

MAHIDA: Oh, nothing so much.

THOMAS: Really, tell me.

(Pause)

THOMAS: Is it something you wrote? A story?

MAHIDA: I don't know.

THOMAS: You don't know if it's a story?

MAHIDA: I struggle sometimes, yes.

(Pause)

THOMAS: I didn't know you brought along a story.

MAHIDA: I was trying to write, yes, in my room at college. When my brother showed up.

THOMAS: Uh huh. I don't suppose you'll let me see it?

MAHIDA: Oh, no.

THOMAS: Why don't you read to me a little?

MAHIDA: No, please.

THOMAS: You know there's no way I'm not going to like it.

MAHIDA: Why don't you show me, please, instead a painting?

THOMAS: Me? A painting?

MAHIDA: Yes. I would love to see something you have done.

THOMAS: I don't have any paintings here.

MAHIDA: There's no drawing here, not even a sketch?

THOMAS: This is my mother's house.

MAHIDA: But you grew up here. You could have left something.

THOMAS: She would have tossed it out.

MAHIDA: No, I don't believe you. I think you are being shy.

THOMAS: I'm not shy.

MAHIDA: Then I do not understand how you cannot show me.

THOMAS: Look, I'll show you when we get to the mainland. I'll show a couple of paintings.

MAHIDA: Good. I'll show you too. On the mainland.

(Pause)

THOMAS: All right. There is something. I remember I gave her something.
(He leaves the porch.)

(MAHIDA looks at her papers, nervous.)

(THOMAS comes back on the porch. He holds a large bowl. He presents it to MAHIDA.)

THOMAS: I made this. I gave it to my mother.

MAHIDA: Yes? You are a potter too?

THOMAS: I can do pottery, yes.

MAHIDA: It's very nice. I like it. Does your mother like it?

THOMAS: Well, sure, it's still on the table. My mother likes what she can put things in. What's literal. Serve vegetables. Mash potatoes.

MAHIDA: I like it no matter what she puts in.

THOMAS: Thank you.

(MAHIDA *holds the bowl.*)

THOMAS: So would you read me a little?
(*Pause*)
I showed you my bowl.

MAHIDA: This is not fair.

THOMAS: Why, because I made a bowl? There's nothing so personal about a bowl?

MAHIDA: Well, no, it's personal. It's very nice. It's lovely to hold, this pot.
Here. Perhaps you should take it back.

THOMAS: Okay.

(THOMAS *takes the bowl. He puts it on a chair.*)

THOMAS: You don't have to read.

MAHIDA: I'm sorry to be so nervous.

THOMAS: You're not nervous. You're just modest.

MAHIDA: No, I'm quite uneasy.

THOMAS: Look, then, let's just wait. You can read later. Maybe on the ferry.

MAHIDA: Okay. The ferry.

(*Pause*)

THOMAS: You sure?

(MAHIDA *fidgets.*)

THOMAS: I'm going to close my eyes, I think. If you read now, you read. Otherwise I'll just think a bit.

We'll think together on this porch. Then we'll get up.
Take a walk out of town.

(He closes his eyes.)

(MAHIDA regards THOMAS.)

(Pause)

MAHIDA: *(Reading)* "When I woke this morning, I saw
there was a stream in my room. And I thought, why is
this stream in my room? I will ask my father. He will
know. And then I realized, no, my father is dead. So I
decided to walk down this stream myself to see where
it led. I followed it down the stairs. It got wider and
wider, until I came to a bridge. At the foot of the stairs.
A stone bridge, which I thought I should cross. There
looked to be some sort of meadow over there. Some
place safe, I thought, from our house. But along the
balustrade of this bridge were ravens. They seemed to
whisper. And I thought, well, they'll fly away if I cross
this bridge. But they didn't. They fell silent instead.
It's quite disturbing to be stared at by so many ravens.
I was halfway across when one of them asked, Where
are you going? And I said, I don't know. There seems
to be a meadow over there. And then the raven said,
Why are you going if you do not know where you will
go? And I said, But I feel I must cross this bridge. I feel
compelled. And so the raven said, Why don't you fly
across this river instead of walking on a bridge? And I
said, I'm sorry, I don't know how to fly. At which point
I looked over the balustrade into the river below. And,
sure enough, I could see the reflection of the bridge
and the sky above, but I couldn't see myself. Where has
my reflection gone, I thought, this whole last year or
so? Who has taken it? And then in the water I noticed
a wolf looking down from the bridge. I turned but next
to me was just the raven. And I asked this bird, Why
is your reflection a wolf in the water? And the bird
said, Why do you have no reflection at all? I said, I

don't know. And the bird said, Then neither do I know. And I said, But, no, I believe you do know. You're not telling. But the raven didn't answer. All the ravens rose and flew away and I was left by myself on that bridge. With no reflection still in the water. And I thought perhaps I must forget about this meadow ahead. I should go back to the house. There's no danger there, I'm sure, nothing which could stalk or haunt. But then I saw the wolf. Up ahead in the meadow. And so I quickly crossed and shouted, Are you the wolf that was the reflection of the raven? But then I noticed there was no shadow to this wolf. I said to him, You have no shadow on the ground. And then I thought, perhaps I'm invisible to this wolf. I see no reflection in his eyes. But then I heard the wolf say, I see you. You think you have no reflection. And I said, I know. I said, Do you think we should travel together? You have no shadow. I have no reflection. Perhaps it would be good, don't you think, to travel for awhile together?"

(Pause)

THOMAS: What does the wolf answer?

MAHIDA: I don't know yet.

THOMAS: Hm. I think they should travel together. Go through that meadow. Find what's on the other side.

MAHIDA: Yes?

THOMAS: I think they're both quite ethereal.

MAHIDA: Ethereal?

THOMAS: Well, they're missing these physical pieces. Like a reflection. There are large cracks, it seems, in what should be a more solid physical appearance. At least on this earth.

(MAHIDA puts aside the papers.)

MAHIDA: I don't know what to do with it. I have all these ideas. I hope when I am more mature I will know.

(Pause)

THOMAS: I'm not sure, maybe, one should trust that raven.

MAHIDA: No?

THOMAS: Isn't it disturbing, she says? To be stared at by ravens?

MAHIDA: Yes, it is.

THOMAS: Well, sure, they eat carrion. Maybe they look at her like she's carrion, or maybe they ate her father, who knows?

MAHIDA: Oh, dear.

THOMAS: I don't mean to be graphic, no. But why trust something that eats carrion while crossing such a bridge? And what if this wolf is actually her own brief momentary reflection and she doesn't know? What if she's running to meet her own reflection over there in the meadow?
I'm sorry. I don't mean to interfere. I'm just saying what I could think.
What passed through my thoughts. About ravens.

MAHIDA: You don't interfere at all. I like what you say about ravens. I will think about it.

THOMAS: It's very beautiful, whatever you do with it. You know that. Very logical.

MAHIDA: Logical?

THOMAS: Sure. There's a logic at work.

MAHIDA: What logic?

THOMAS: A basic logic, you know that. Everything makes sense. What the raven says, if you trust it or not. How the wolf appears. What this danger might be. Everything, I think.

(Pause)

MAHIDA: Well, thank you. Thank you for saying that.

THOMAS: I mean that.

MAHIDA: Yes?

THOMAS: It makes beautiful sense.

(MAHIDA smiles. She shifts awkwardly.)

Scene Four

(The living room. Late morning)

(The sound of knocking)

(Pause. More knocking)

(EDNA appears at the stairs. She regards the front door. She goes to it. She opens it.)

(RAMIN stands outside on the steps.)

EDNA: Yes? May I help you?

(No response)

EDNA: I said, May I help you?
Do you speak English?

(Pause)

RAMIN: I am here to see my sister.

EDNA: Your what?

RAMIN: I have a sister.

EDNA: Oh, really?

RAMIN: In this house, yes.

EDNA: Ah.

(Pause)

You must be Mahida's brother. Who's visiting this country.

(Pause)

I thought you went back already. On the ferry. The ferry yesterday. That's what I was told.

(RAMIN steps through the door.)

EDNA: Here. What are you doing? I haven't invited you in.

RAMIN: I am come for Mahida.

EDNA: No, we haven't done talking at the door.

RAMIN: I will talk here.

EDNA: Really?

RAMIN: I want to see my sister.

EDNA: I see. Well, she's not here.

RAMIN: Of course, she is.

EDNA: No, I'm afraid she's gone for a walk. You seem to have missed her.

RAMIN: What walk?

EDNA: What do you mean, What walk? She and my son went out the back. For a walk.

RAMIN: Out the back. Very well.

EDNA: Yes, some time ago. Who knows when they'll be back.

RAMIN: I shall wait then.

EDNA: What?

RAMIN: I should like to wait. For my sister. For her return.

EDNA: What, in here?

RAMIN: Yes, I am very good at waiting. Very patient, you'll see. You will hardly notice. How quiet I will be as all the pictures on your wall. As these knickknacks I see on the shelf. I will be very still. Like the carpet on your floor. Like a calm before the storm. I will be only in the periphery of your eye. Almost invisible, I'm sure.

(Pause)

EDNA: Well, fine, I suppose. Take a seat over there. Till your sister comes back.

(RAMIN takes a seat by the wall in the living room.)

(EDNA closes the front door.)

(Pause)

EDNA: May I get you something? Some tea, I suppose.

RAMIN: No, thank you.

EDNA: I see. Perhaps a biscuit then? A bun or muffin?

RAMIN: No, thank you. No muffin.

(EDNA takes a seat in the living room. She regards RAMIN.)

EDNA: You're not going to be surly, are you now? In this house? Because that's one thing we can't have here. Any more surliness, you understand?

(No response)

EDNA: You certainly seem rather different from your sister.

(Pause)

I asked your sister about her siblings. Over there in your land. At breakfast this morning. And she told me what a wonderful toddler you were. Of all her siblings you were the most playful. Attentive to your mother. That's what she told. Of course, that probably seems all rather long ago to you. Distant. You look so big now. And my son too. He was once all playful and silly. Quite the toddler, I remember.

(Pause)

Your sister told me how she was named. Got that name of hers, Mahida. Do you remember? After a close business associate of your father. Some man he worked with from India.

She says your father was very progressive. Quite generous.

(Pause)

Your sister told me how talkative and charming the people can be in your land. What good hosts they are. How they love to converse. About metaphysics and history. About poetry. What pride they take in making sure you're comfortable as a guest in their home, or just in general in their land. Your sister says it's amazing, it is, the misconceptions we have of what actually happens over there in the land you're from.

(Pause)

You're not married, are you?

(Pause)

If you expect to sit waiting in my house, you'll have to answer some questions. Make a little conversation. Or else I'm afraid I'll have to ask you to leave. Wait out there somewhere in the street for your sister.

RAMIN: I'm not married.

EDNA: Hm. But your two other sisters, they're both married? Back in Iran.

RAMIN: Yes. They are married.

EDNA: That's nice. And yourself? Will you marry?

RAMIN: Allah willing.

EDNA: Pardon?

RAMIN: If Allah wishes.

EDNA: Of course. If Allah wishes. On the other hand, I was just wondering if you had a personal preference.

RAMIN: My personal preference is immaterial.

EDNA: Pardon?

RAMIN: I do not prefer personally.

EDNA: Oh?

(Pause)

What are you doing, by the way, in our country?

RAMIN: I have come for my sister.

EDNA: Really? All the way here to pick up your sister?

RAMIN: Yes.

EDNA: No other reason, then, for your visit here?

RAMIN: I will find my sister.

(Pause)

EDNA: Mahida tells me you actually go to a university in Tehran.

RAMIN: No, actually, I travel.

EDNA: Travel?

RAMIN: I am travelling, yes.

EDNA: Oh? So you're not going to that university in Tehran? As your father asked you?

RAMIN: No. I am studying now sometimes in Lebanon. I have visited too Haqqania.

EDNA: Pardon?

RAMIN: *(Slowly)* Haqqania. It is a madrassa they have.

EDNA: Ah. A religious school, you mean?

RAMIN: A most famous one, yes.

EDNA: I see. But your sister says they don't have madrassas in Iran.

RAMIN: No, in fact. It is near the Khyber Pass. In Pakistan.

EDNA: Oh. Pakistan.

RAMIN: Yes.

EDNA: But your sister said this morning Iranians don't generally go on visits to Pakistan.

RAMIN: They don't visit, you say?

EDNA: Well, I don't know. She was explaining about Shiites and Sunnis, I believe. How hard it is for you to mingle, or something.

RAMIN: I see.

EDNA: But you go anyway to Pakistan, do you, or Lebanon? You mingle, yes, or visit over there?

(No response)

EDNA: Well, I'm sorry, yes, I am. All that stuff going on over there in your part of the world. Pakistan, the Middle East. All that turmoil. We're trying to do our best, you know. Our level headed best, I can assure you, to catch you up with all we've discovered to be good in this world.

(Pause)

Are you glowering at me?

(No response)

EDNA: You seem to glower. I can't be sure.

RAMIN: I think you should be more careful. What you say.

EDNA: I should?

RAMIN: Oh, yes.

EDNA: Really? But this is my house. I should say what I think in here.

RAMIN: Yes. But I am here too. In your house.

EDNA: Well, as a guest.

RAMIN: You can call me, if you like, a guest.

EDNA: You're not?

RAMIN: I am waiting for my sister.

EDNA: Well, that's a guest.

RAMIN: If you wish.

EDNA: Well, what else could you be? An intruder?

RAMIN: I could be, yes, an intruder. Or a guest. As you wish.

EDNA: What are you trying to be? Rather enigmatical with me?

RAMIN: No, I am a guest, as you say. Or an intruder, who knows? And outside this house, of course, is eternity. What we know will never end. The big wind of what is to come.

EDNA: The big wind, eh?

RAMIN: Yes, I believe so. These things which mingle now, as you say.
Become compounded perhaps.

(Pause)

EDNA: So. What do they teach you, then, in Lebanon? Or in your travels? What is it they make you learn?

(No response)

EDNA: They busy teaching you, I suppose, some more perfect world, I imagine? Than whatever we've managed to arrange for ourselves here? You learn for yourselves, do you, what used to be, what once was in that bygone civilization of yours?

(No response)

EDNA: Is it true you memorize that Koran of yours? Every hour of the day. Each moment you have that book open. Is that what all that rocking is about, memorizing? The one book, I hear, on your reading list. Besides whatever else you're up to.

(Pause)

RAMIN: You should learn to think before you speak. It would be better, I'm sure.

EDNA: You say, think? I think.

RAMIN: No, I see no evidence of such thinking. Before you speak.

EDNA: Well, how would you know? I see no evidence from you either.

RAMIN: *(Smiling)* No?

EDNA: Of any thinking, no, as you say, before you speak. I imagine you're probably rather inculcated, in fact.

RAMIN: Inculcated?

EDNA: Oh, yes.

RAMIN: Well, that is funny. You to say I am inculcated.

EDNA: Well, yes, ours is a thinking society.

RAMIN: Oh, you think so?

EDNA: Pardon?

RAMIN: I said, Do you really think so? This is such a thinking society? What you do to this world, you call that such thinking?

(Pause)

EDNA: Listen. Mahida told me herself you don't think. Never have. You just embrace. Embrace something or other. Like soccer. You had the talent to be a soccer star, she said. Or the imagination to be an artist, or a singer. You're like a free spirit, I hear. Some kind of ball of fire. But as soon as it gets hard, or your father said something, you jump to something else. That's what your own sister says.

So don't talk to me about thinking, how our country is thinking.

(Pause)

(Restless) I'll say this for Thomas. At least he's stubborn, that's for sure. He's always wanted to draw and nothing I've said has ever deterred, or given him pause. Nothing I could say about his father's example, or his uncle. These people who never think, you know. How to support a family. Just abdicate from any thought like that. And Thomas has the same refusal. To give any thought to what's practical, what's real, you know, in this world. And why that university he went to gave him all that support, you know, those loans and scholarships, I'll never understand.

I'll never understand the purpose of any of that.

(She has exited into the dining room.)

(Pause. She returns.)

You sure you wouldn't want some tea?

That bun or muffin?

(No response)

(EDNA stands by a small table. She opens a drawer. She closes it.)

EDNA: So, tell me. I'm curious. What is it about that one book on your reading list?

That Koran of yours, you say.

RAMIN: I read other things.

EDNA: Oh, yes?

RAMIN: In fact, what you call the Old Testament. The New Testament too. I read all prophets. Moses, Isaiah, Jeremiah, Ezekiel, Jesus, peace be upon them. They are all prophets. Before Muhammad, peace and blessings upon him, who is the Final Prophet.

EDNA: I see.

RAMIN: Do you memorize too your scripture?

EDNA: Do I memorize?

RAMIN: Yes, what do you commit to memory? What thoughts do you wish to attain?

EDNA: Attain?

RAMIN: Learn by heart, yes.

EDNA: Oh. Well, I've memorized, of course, the 23rd Psalm. The Lord's Prayer. I'm particularly fond, I believe, of the 121st Psalm: "I will lift up mine eyes unto the hills, from whence cometh my help. My help cometh from the Lord, which made heaven and earth."

RAMIN: Hm. Then you must know the Book of Samuel.

EDNA: Samuel? Well, yes, of course.

RAMIN: I, too, as a boy, heard the voice of God.

EDNA: The voice of God?

RAMIN: Like Samuel.

EDNA: Oh, you mean like Samuel when he was a little boy. Woken up like that three times by the voice of God saying, Samuel?

RAMIN: Yes.

EDNA: That happened to you, that voice of God? When you were a toddler.

RAMIN: Yes. When I was little.

EDNA: Oh. And what did you do? Were you like Samuel who ran, you know, into the bedroom of Eli the priest, saying, Here I am. You called? And Eli saying, No, I didn't call. Go back to bed.

RAMIN: Yes. Exactly like Samuel.

EDNA: Hm. And whose room did you run into? When you heard such a voice?

RAMIN: I thought it was my mother who spoke.

EDNA: Oh? She told you, like Eli, go back and answer God?

RAMIN: Yes, she did.

EDNA: But how could that be? How could God sound to you like your mother, like some woman?

RAMIN: God can do as He pleases.

(Pause)

EDNA: Hm. Must be nice, I suppose. Imagining like that you hear the voice of God. As a toddler.
Anything in particular, you imagine, he told you? This voice of God. When you finally answered.

(No response)

EDNA: Nothing you'd divulge, I suppose.

(No response)

EDNA: You do have a rather nasty look sometimes. Just a glimmer, or glint, that's all. I'm sure you can't mean it. At least not in somebody else's house.

(RAMIN stands. He goes to a window.)

EDNA: I thought it was Allah who talked to you people. Not God.

RAMIN: Allah is the name of God among Muslims. And among Arab Christians.

EDNA: Yes, right.

RAMIN: I am honored to be the agent of Allah. Or you can call him God. Who will destroy all misconceptions concerning Him.

EDNA: Well, yes.
I believe that too, actually. About misconceptions. What He will destroy. We're in for quite a bit of destruction, I do believe. Any moment now.

RAMIN: Ah. I'm surprised.

EDNA: Really, by what?

RAMIN: To hear you believe that. I thought there was no God anymore in this country. It is a post-Christian society, I hear them say.

EDNA: Well, that's nonsense.

RAMIN: Really? You see God here? In your country?

EDNA: Of course, I do. There's lots of God in our country. In Him we trust. It's right there on our money.

RAMIN: *(Grinning)* Ah, your money.

EDNA: What's so funny?

RAMIN: God is in all this your money buys? There's God in your television programs? Your Hollywood? Your advertisements on your buses or magazines? These photographs and posters with young men and women, even boys and girls, touching each other while they wear only underpants? This is God to you? To advertise like this? Everywhere I walk in your country, everywhere I look, I see something to make people think of sex, or to take a drug. To suggest these things. This is what you want your children to see? How they should grow up? With all this false allurement?

EDNA: Well, no, of course not.

RAMIN: This enticement? You might as well hand your children now a new alphabet coloring book. The letter "A" could be a picture of adultery or anal sex.

EDNA: Oh.

RAMIN: How to do these things. The letter "B" could be bellyache or buggery. "C" would be copulation or cancer. This would at least be truthful. How can you teach a child to be deaf and blind to what is all around? What surrounds them in your country? What must surely infect how they think, what they choose. And

what you now want to surround all the rest of the
world with.

EDNA: The rest of the world?

RAMIN: Oh, yes. You think what you do stops here on
these shores? This is your freedom? Your sprawl? To
spread out across the whole world? To change what
we see in our own lands, what is in our own thoughts,
or the thoughts of our children and women?
Hah.
This is your supply side economics? Your foreign
investment laws?
This is more than an invasion, I think. Some soldiers
who come by for a century or so. No, this is an attempt
to remake the world. To change forever the very face
of the earth. The ground we stand on. To manipulate
all the minds of men and to brush aside all opposing
culture. To make us all in your image. What your land
here has become.

(Pause)

EDNA: Hm. I do believe you sound rather resentful.

RAMIN: Resentful, you think?

EDNA: Yes. Rather excessive, I would say, in your
criticisms. Just because we have a few aberrations
here in our country, some misconceptions, as you
say, that doesn't mean there's no God, no. Every
place on earth, every land, has problems with its
misconceivers. Misguided politicians, or leaders,
you know that yourself. You have, or those sheikhs
have, over there seventy-five offspring. Who else is
spreading themselves like that all across the world?
It's a matter of degree. To what degree is a nation of
people misconceived. And as far as that goes, for all
the problems, there is no question, I'm afraid, what's
Western is the least, by far, misconceived. On this

earth. In comparison, everything else is positively benighted. This country is the light of the world. What we have here. And if that light is misconstrued, or made murky, by certain reprobates in our land, nevertheless, this nation is still the basis, in fact, upon which the human race is most likely to proceed. Otherwise it's all dogs and darkness and barbarians out there. It's as simple as that. And if we don't pay attention to that, what's howling out there at our gates, well, then I'm sorry, we're in for it all over again, another one of those huge collapses, an apocalyptic dark age, I say.

(Pause)

Well, now, you've got me started, you have. Defending my country. Right here in my own house. My very home.

(She regards him.)

Yes, as I say. You do seem to have a rather nasty look sometimes. Just a glint, that's all. And then it disappears.

Are you aware of it?

This look of yours? Which then seems to disappear?

(Pause)

RAMIN: You too, I think, have a nasty look. A glint yourself.

EDNA: A nasty look?

RAMIN: Oh, yes. Very hard and narrow. Like a cowboy, I think. When there were still Indians in this land.

EDNA: We have Indians.

RAMIN: Perhaps.

EDNA: What do you mean, Perhaps? What kind of talk is that, perhaps?

(No response)

EDNA: Well, you know what I think, perhaps. I think, perhaps, I have had enough company for now. I think, also perhaps, I have no idea why you're in this country. What could bring you here. After all this talk with you, in my very own home, I still have, perhaps, no idea at all what it is you're doing here.

RAMIN: I'm waiting for my sister.

EDNA: Yes, you said. But I still can't fathom why.

RAMIN: You can't fathom?

EDNA: No, I can't. I've lost patience with this, with what can't be fathomed. All this perhaps. And I would like it now, in fact, for you to leave. If you're going to wait for your sister like this, perhaps you just better do it outside.

RAMIN: I don't think so, no.

EDNA: Really?

RAMIN: It's awkward actually, outside.

EDNA: Awkward outside?

RAMIN: Yes, standing around. You know this.

EDNA: Why? Because there are people out there, maybe passing by?

RAMIN: Yes. That is so.

EDNA: Well, maybe I should write you a note then. Would you like a note?

RAMIN: A note?

EDNA: Yes, a piece of paper. I'll write something on a paper, saying, yes, it's okay for you to wait outside until your sister comes back.
(*She heads for a small table. She opens a drawer.*)
Would you like that? If I gave you a note?

(*No response*)

EDNA: A note, yes, in case anyone asks? Should someone want to know what you're doing out there. You could show my note.

RAMIN: I think that would be unwise.

EDNA: What would be unwise?

RAMIN: To think I could accept such a note.

EDNA: Oh? You're telling me what's unwise? Right here in my own house?

RAMIN: Yes, that could be.

EDNA: Well. There's really not much choice here, is there? Either you wait outside with a note. Or without a note.
Did you hear?

(No response)

EDNA: Listen. I think you should understand that you just can't come into someone's house, for whatever reason, and then lurk around and harbor these nasty looks of yours. At least not in this country.
We don't put up with that sort of thing.

(Pause)

(She removes a revolver from the drawer of the table.)
I will ask you now, one more time, to leave my house.

(No response)

(EDNA levels the revolver at RAMIN.)

EDNA: You are an intruder in my house. I will call you an intruder. I will tell the sheriff, and everyone I know in this town, you intruded into my house.
I will do this.
If you do not leave right now.

(RAMIN watches EDNA. He does not move.)

Scene Five

(The living room. Noontime)

(RAMIN sits in a chair by the wall, waiting. He stares at the knickknacks in the room. He eats a muffin. EDNA is gone. The front door opens.)

(THOMAS and MAHIDA enter. THOMAS holds a sketch book. They see RAMIN. RAMIN stands.)

(Pause)

MAHIDA: Ramin?

(No response)

MAHIDA: Ramin. This is Thomas.

THOMAS: *(To RAMIN)* How do you do?

(No response)

MAHIDA: Ramin, Thomas is the man who offered to help me last night. When I was left alone on this island. Perhaps you saw. There was no ferry. Not even a hotel, or inn, for me to stay.
And so Thomas talked to me and told me later to come to this house. It is his mother's house. Thomas is visiting his mother. I could be allowed, he said, to sleep on the couch right here. And so I slept. I had a good rest. A good breakfast too with Thomas and his mother. I read to Thomas some of my writing, what I told you I was working on. And Thomas has showed me some drawing. Yes, Thomas, you were drawing?

THOMAS: Sure.
(He steps forward with his sketch book. He opens it. He lays it on the coffee table nearby.)

MAHIDA: Yes. I like how Thomas can draw. Thomas and I are back just now, in fact, from a walk outside of town to a hilltop above the ocean.

Pretty soon we're hoping to take the ferry. Thomas has offered to make sure I get back safely to the university. I have a class in a couple of hours.

(Pause)

Those are the facts.

(Pause)

What is it you're thinking?

(No response)

(THOMAS goes to the dining room. He exits.)

(RAMIN goes to MAHIDA's suitcase by the door. He picks it up.)

(THOMAS appears again at the dining room door.)

THOMAS: *(To RAMIN)* Where's my mother?

(No response)

MAHIDA: Ramin, where is Thomas' mother?

RAMIN: His mother has gone out.

THOMAS: Out?

RAMIN: *(Putting down the suitcase)* Yes.

THOMAS: That's not possible. My mother would never go out. With a stranger in the house.

RAMIN: I am not a stranger.

THOMAS: What?

RAMIN: I have introduced myself to your mother.

THOMAS: My mother would still not go out. She would not leave you here.

RAMIN: Oh, why not?

THOMAS: Look, it's not just you. It's anybody. My mother is very particular. There's no way she would leave you here. Someone she just met. My mother likes to hover. If a carpenter or plumber comes in, she hovers. The electrician. She has this house specifically so she can hover over whoever comes in.

I know. I'm her son. It's embarrassing.

(Pause)

RAMIN: Well, that may be so. You are embarrassed. But she went out. She went out, she said, for food. We need lots of food, she said.

THOMAS: Lots of food, huh?

RAMIN: I believe so. So many people now for lunch.

(THOMAS circles the room. He stands by the front door.)

THOMAS: My mother is way too suspicious. Too territorial to ever just go out for food. Without locking up this whole house. You see each of these windows here? These windows would not be open, no, if my mother left the house. Because it might rain. It'll drizzle. They'd be locked. This light too would not be on.

(THOMAS turns off the light by the door.)

THOMAS: And as for you, she would have asked you, I know, to wait out on the street. Until she came back.

(Pause)

MAHIDA: Ramin. Where is Thomas's mother?

RAMIN: *(Shrugs)* She went out.

(THOMAS circles the room again. He stands by the dining room door.)

MAHIDA: *(Keeping her eyes on RAMIN)* Thomas?

THOMAS: What?

MAHIDA: Please don't get angry.

THOMAS: What do you mean, Don't get angry?

MAHIDA: I want you not to get angry.

THOMAS: Something's wrong, I think, with my mother.

MAHIDA: Please. We must think very carefully now.

THOMAS: What?

MAHIDA: I said, Don't get angry.

THOMAS: Don't get angry? Am I getting angry?

MAHIDA: Yes. I think so.

(Pause)

THOMAS: Sure. Sure, that's probably all this is. Just getting angry.

RAMIN: Oh. I'm very sorry. So sorry.
I forgot. She left a note.

(RAMIN takes a folded piece of paper out of his pocket. He hands it to MAHIDA.)

RAMIN: Please. Show his mother's note.

(MAHIDA goes to THOMAS. She hands him the paper.)

(THOMAS opens it.)

THOMAS: *(Reading)* "I've gone out for food. Make yourselves at home. Ramin will be joining us for lunch. Mother."

(Pause)

Are you toying with us?

RAMIN: Toying?

THOMAS: Why did you just now show this note?

RAMIN: It was in my pocket.

THOMAS: She gave it to you to put in your pocket?

RAMIN: No, of course. I believe she left it over there by the table. By the light that was turned on. But, as you can see, all the windows are open. She left them open. There was a breeze and I saw the paper blow to the ground. And I wondered how will her son see this note on the floor. So without much thinking, I folded it up and put it in my pocket. To keep it safe. Until just now when I remembered.

I'm sorry. I understand now why you could not believe she went shopping.

(He regards THOMAS.*)*

You still don't believe? Your mother went shopping? You shouldn't look so wary. You should learn to trust better, I think. All the peoples of this world.

(Pause)

MAHIDA: *(In Persian)* Ramin. What have you come here to do?

(No response)

MAHIDA: What is it, Ramin? You have come here to do?

RAMIN: What have I come to do?

MAHIDA: Yes.

RAMIN: I am only here, you know this. To bring you back.

MAHIDA: You expect me to come back?

RAMIN: Yes. We should both go back.

MAHIDA: You have no other business?

RAMIN: What business? What business could there be for me in this country?

MAHIDA: And what about what has happened here?

RAMIN: Nothing has happened here.

MAHIDA: No?

RAMIN: No, his mother will be back, safe and sound, I told you.

(Pause)

MAHIDA: I see. Why should I believe you?

You want me to believe, don't you? If I should come back with you.

(No response)

MAHIDA: You told me in the car yesterday you have left university. And I don't know if it is true what you say, but it makes me sad. To realize you would even think to go like this against our father's wishes.

(Pause)

If you are going now to be a cleric someplace, what do you expect me to believe? That you, Ramin, would spend so many years memorizing and learning to interpret the Holy Book?

(No response)

MAHIDA: I fear what you may have heard. What you were told perhaps somewhere. How to skip all this study. Gain God's favor. Some other way.

(Pause)

Ramin.

RAMIN: Yes, dear sister?

MAHIDA: What is it you want me to think? I am confused how you are here.

RAMIN: I know very well what you should think.

MAHIDA: Oh?

RAMIN: You will be sorry, I know, to bother with such questions to your brother.

MAHIDA: Ramin.

RAMIN: You will be sorry soon, I'm sure.

(Pause)

MAHIDA: How have you become like this? So much the opposite of our father?

(She goes to the coffee table. She closes the sketch book.)

Last night, Ramin, as I lay on this couch, I could not
sleep. Thinking of you. Thinking what has happened to
my brother? Who is speaking to him? Who could these
people be? And do they love Ramin the way I love
Ramin? How I have always loved him?

(*Pause*)

I prayed to know you are safe. I prayed this with all
my heart. Until I realized, yes. You came to see me.
My brother put aside some trouble, or plan. To see me.
How could I not see this before?
That is how I finally fell asleep. How I got rest.
But then I became worried again. Today outside on
the walk. I couldn't keep my mind still. And so I asked
Thomas, Please, leave me alone. I must be alone for
awhile on the top of this hill. And so I looked out alone
across the ocean and once again I wanted to know,
with all my heart, that no harm can come to you. You
are safe. And then, Ramin, the sweetest thought came. I
saw Mother reading from the Book of Samuel. We were
children. And you ran the next night to our mother,
saying, Did you call? I heard you call? And our father,
Ramin, he was touched, I believe. That his son could
confuse his own need for his parents' attention for the
voice of God.

(*Pause*)

I don't know why, Ramin. I thought of that while I
stood, looking out across the ocean. Why it gave me
peace. Made me realize there is no lie here on earth
which can possibly touch you. Turn you away from
who you are. What you are created to be.

(*Pause*)

You may not hear me now, I know, Ramin.
But I can pray, I know, you will hear perhaps later.

(MAHIDA *reaches for* RAMIN. *He steps away.*)

RAMIN: Well, perhaps, we should all sit. Make conversation, then. While we wait all together. For this man's mother.

(He sits.)

(Pause)

No one will care to sit?

MAHIDA: Ramin?

RAMIN: Yes, dear sister?

MAHIDA: Where is Thomas' mother?

RAMIN: I told you she is shopping.

MAHIDA: Please, Ramin.

RAMIN: It is true. You would doubt your brother's word?

MAHIDA: Yes, Ramin. I doubt.

RAMIN: You must not doubt what I know is best for you. What is true. What you will thank me for later.

MAHIDA: *(Gently)* Ramin, I will only thank you first to tell me where his mother has gone.

(RAMIN abruptly stands, lifting a tray from the coffee table with him. He heaves the tray across the room. It crashes into the shelf of knickknacks. In the confusion, he swiftly steps forward and seizes THOMAS by the wrist completely surprising him. He twists THOMAS' forearm and pushes down on his elbow. THOMAS gasps. RAMIN stares into THOMAS' face. He walks THOMAS, bent over and helpless, slowly around the room.)

RAMIN: How do you like it? How do you like it, my fellow American? How swiftly I can cast aside all your defenses. How I too can invade your home. Where you hope to live. How I am come now right here into the heart of your country. Like you have slipped into the heart of mine.

MAHIDA: *(Quietly)* Ramin.

RAMIN: *(To* THOMAS*)* How do you like it? To be
this close to one small face of what will cause your
destruction? Tear apart all the fabric of how you live.
You have no way ever now to protect yourself from
this.

MAHIDA: Ramin.

RAMIN: *(To* THOMAS*)* No way to close every crack from
which I could come. No way to dismount now the back
of this tiger you ride.

*(*MAHIDA *reaches forward and touches* RAMIN *on the
shoulder. He releases* THOMAS *and takes* MAHIDA *with one
hand by the throat.)*

*(*THOMAS *slips to the ground in shock and pain.)*

RAMIN: *(Hissing)* Mahida!

MAHIDA: *(Struggling to breathe)* Yes?

RAMIN: *(Hissing)* You must never doubt what I know is
true. You will thank me later for what I know is true.

MAHIDA: *(Breathing)* Yes?

*(*RAMIN *releases* MAHIDA. *She slides to the floor, her scarf
slipping off.)*

*(*RAMIN *leans down into her face.)*

RAMIN: *(Slowly)* I will no longer waste my time now. In
what life remains, with a sister who will not listen.

*(*RAMIN *goes to the front door. He hesitates. He takes*
EDNA*'s revolver out of his pocket. He lays it on a
windowsill. He exits.)*

(Pause)

(Both MAHIDA *and* THOMAS *continue to lie on the ground.)*

MAHIDA: Thomas?

THOMAS: *(Faintly)* Yes?

(MAHIDA *sits up, holding her throat.*)

MAHIDA: I think your mother is upstairs, Thomas. Ramin has left your mother upstairs.

THOMAS: *(Faintly)* Yes?

MAHIDA: You are all right?

THOMAS: *(Faintly)* Yes, I am.

(MAHIDA *stands. She goes to* THOMAS. *She helps him sit up.*)

MAHIDA: Thomas? May I go upstairs? May I find your mother?

THOMAS: *(Faintly)* Okay.

(MAHIDA *takes* THOMAS' *hand. She holds it.*)

MAHIDA: Thank you, Thomas, so much. You listened to me. Thank you.

THOMAS: *(Faintly)* I did?

MAHIDA: You did not get angry. Thank you.

THOMAS: *(Faintly)* You're welcome.

(MAHIDA *stands. She goes to the stairs.*)

Scene Six

(*Two days later. Early evening. The upper passenger deck of a ferry.*)

(EDNA *sits on a bench. Her face is partially wrapped. Her jaw appears to have been broken.* MAHIDA *sits with her, holding hands. She has a sketch book and pencil beside her.*)

(*Some distance away* THOMAS *leans against a railing, looking down at the water.*)

(*Pause*)

MAHIDA: Thank you for coming with us. We did not want to leave you alone.

(EDNA *nods.*)

MAHIDA: Thank you also, so much, for understanding how sorry I am, please, for what Ramin has done to you.
How my brother came like that to your house.

(EDNA *nods.*)

MAHIDA: I am sorry too for all those questions. How they detained us.
I am very sorry for these last two days.
I know. I have said this.

(EDNA *nods.*)

MAHIDA: They will find my brother. Or he will find himself, I know. He cannot escape what is best.
(*Pause. She shifts awkwardly on the bench.*)

(EDNA *holds out her hand. She takes the sketch book and pencil. She writes on the back cover. She hands it to* MAHIDA.)

(MAHIDA *reads the cover. She looks up at* EDNA.)

MAHIDA: (*Surprised*) Thank you.
Oh, thank you for writing this.
(*Pause*)
I, too, am thinking so much.
I, too, must begin again.
(*Pause*)
You have spoken sometimes of toddlers. How your son was once a toddler.
I have heard you.
I remember Ramin when he first learned to walk. I would hold his hand. I helped him cross the room.
(*Pause*)

This morning I remembered we were on bicycles once.
Ramin went past me going down a hill. And I saw
his front wheel begin to wobble. It wobbled more and
more until I saw him crash at the bottom of the hill.
Ramin was okay.
But I will always remember how helpless I felt going
down the hill. When I saw his wheel in front wobble
like that.
(Pause)
I want to tell you this is the Ramin I know.
There is a Ramin I trust. Ramin I love and adore.
And if he has now wandered somehow across some
boundary. Some borderline to consider some things
I never thought possible. Whatever the reason is and
whatever in the world could prompt such things.
Whatever, or whoever, could propel him, nothing can
take away from me, or anyone, the Ramin who could
look up at me after crashing his bicycle like that at the
bottom of a hill and say, "Dear sister, how can you
weep like so?"
It was Ramin who had no care for himself. No care for
cuts or bruises, any broken bones.
It was Ramin who comforted me because I was
weeping.

(Pause)

(THOMAS *looks up from the railing. He looks out across the
water.)*

(EDNA *and* MAHIDA *watch* THOMAS.)

MAHIDA: May I ask you?
Have you seen what Thomas has drawn?
What he drew this afternoon while we waited for you
at the doctor's?

(EDNA *shakes her head.)*

MAHIDA: I like it very much. What your son can draw.

(Pause)

Here. I will show you. What Thomas has drawn.

(MAHIDA opens the sketch book. She holds it open for EDNA.)

MAHIDA: Do you see? There is a wolf and a little
girl with a shadow. This wolf has no shadow on the
ground like the girl. They are standing before a high
stone wall. At the end of a meadow. I think they have
come to a place where they can go no further. Their
way is blocked by a locked gate in this wall.
See the gate with a lock?
But in the tree over here, above the wolf, is a bird. A
friendly white dove who has the shadow of a raven.
Right here in the air above the wolf. And in the beak
of the dove, she has a key. But in this shadow, the
shadow of the raven, there are two more keys. Maybe
even more.

(Pause)

What do you think of that?
How your son can draw?

(EDNA nods.)

(THOMAS turns from the railing.)

THOMAS: *(Softly)* Mahida?

MAHIDA: *(Hearing him)* Yes, Thomas?

THOMAS: Come, please. Come bring my mother.
Come and see.

MAHIDA: Yes?

THOMAS: Come see how quiet. How still.
Let's come and see this ocean.

(MAHIDA stands. She helps EDNA up.)

(MAHIDA and EDNA walk toward THOMAS.)

(THOMAS *takes* EDNA's *arm.* MAHIDA *takes her hand.*
THOMAS, EDNA *and* MAHIDA *stand by the railing. They
look out across the ocean.*)

END OF PLAY

PLAYWRIGHT'S NOTE

Some years ago I was sitting in the International
Arrivals Building at Newark Airport. I was waiting
for friends to arrive from Europe. As I waited for their
plane to disembark, I watched the many different
people walk past me headed for various gates,
counters, or exits. There were individuals from all over
the world. I sat watching, just as I used to when I was a
boy and was first sent off to school in Great Britain. At
the time my parents lived in Milan, Italy. And before
that we lived in Beirut, Lebanon. And then we were in
Japan and also in Germany. I spent half of fifth grade
in the United States, that was it. The bulk of my school
education was in Lebanon, England, and Switzerland,
until I finally showed up on the shores of this country
for college.

Sitting that day in Newark International Arrivals I
suddenly had this thought. I thought, this is my home
town. These are my people, these are my villagers.
Right here in this airport lobby is where I feel I grew
up. That thought has stayed with me.

I've always felt somewhat a foreigner, or a traveler,
in my own country. I have no home town. I've lived,
officially, in New York City, upstate New York,
Pennsylvania, and now New Hampshire. I've been a
visiting theatre artist in different cities and towns. But
to this day I feel somewhat like a foreigner just getting
off the plane. Still startled by such things as the intense

consumerism evident in our culture, the violent images we seek to entertain ourselves by, the aggressiveness of our advertising, the intense and powerful focus we sometimes exert on the mere surface of things, and the accompanying, almost brutal, disregard sometimes for the side, or ripple, effects of what we think or do.

I am both deeply proud and embarrassed to be a citizen of the United States of America. Our nation was founded – it could not have been founded, in fact, without certain compromises being accepted by both our more northerly states and more southerly states in the language of our Constitution. We have struggled to resolve and break free from those compromises ever since. And there have been times when we have looked bad, or deeply confused, in the eyes of the rest of the world.

But I feel strongly there have been genuine and sustained flashes of an authentic, invigorating sense of democracy, a deeper sense of humanity and unity, a more honest, discerning justice, amongst our people than is evident in most of the rest of the world at present. And of course there have been backlashes against these breakthroughs in our perceptions of our fellow beings.

I feel, like many of us in this country, that we are caught right now in a crossfire between extremes on our right and on our left. I feel a danger that creative, insightful, nuanced, compassionate thought and feeling could be lost in such a crossfire.

And this crossfire appears to be happening all across our world.

And now I realize how much I've always wanted to write such a play—where two characters, from such utterly different nations, from such divergent

perceptions, finally get together on a ferry going across
a distant body of water.

Peterborough Players, Peterborough, New Hampshire, 2019

www.ingramcontent.com/pod-product-compliance
Lightning Source LLC
Chambersburg PA
CBHW052211090426
42741CB00010B/2496